Stephen W. (Stephen Wheeler) Downey

The Immortals

Stephen W. (Stephen Wheeler) Downey

The Immortals

ISBN/EAN: 9783337048488

Printed in Europe, USA, Canada, Australia, Japan

Cover: Foto ©ninafisch / pixelio.de

More available books at **www.hansebooks.com**

THE IMMORTALS.

ARGUMENT.

OF

HON. STEPHEN W. DOWNEY,

OF WYOMING TERRITORY,

IN THE

HOUSE OF REPRESENTATIVES,

TUESDAY, APRIL 13, 1880,

ON

A BILL PROVIDING FOR CERTAIN PAINTINGS ON THE WALLS OF THE NATIONAL CAPITOL.

Phantasmagoria, farewell! I leave
Thee now to nurse thy offspring in the beams
That never fade, and warmth that never chills.

ARGUMENT

OF

HON. STEPHEN W. DOWNEY,

OF WYOMING TERRITORY,

IN THE HOUSE OF REPRESENTATIVES,

Tuesday, April 13, 1880.

Mr. DOWNEY said :

Mr. SPEAKER: On the 12th day of April, A. D. 1880, I introduced the following bill, namely :

A bill providing for certain paintings on the walls of the National Capitol.

Whereas the people of the United States are a Christian people and firmly believe in God the Father Almighty, Maker of heaven and earth ; and in Jesus Christ His only Son our Lord; who was conceived by the Holy Ghost, born of the Virgin Mary; suffered under Pontius Pilate, was crucified, dead and buried ; He descended into hell, the third day He rose from the dead : He ascended into heaven, and sitteth on the right hand of God the Father Almighty ; from thence He shall come to judge the quick and the dead ; and believe in the Holy Ghost, the holy catholic church, the communion of saints, the forgiveness of sins, the resurrection of the body, and the life everlasting. Amen: Therefore,

Be it enacted by the Senate and House of Representatives of the United States of America in Congress assembled, That the sum of $500,000, or so much thereof as may be necessary, be, and the same is hereby, appropriated, out of any funds in the Treasury not otherwise appropriated, to be expended under the direction of the Architect of the Capitol, to commemorate in suitable paintings by the great living artists of this century upon the walls of the National Capitol the birth, life, death, and resurrection of our Saviour Jesus Christ, as told in the four gospels of Matthew, Mark, Luke, and John.

In support of its provisions I have the honor to offer the following argument, entitled :

THE IMMORTALS.

Dedicated to the Congress of the United States.

"For, go back to the beginning of ages, examine all nations, read the history of kingdoms and empires, listen to those who return from the most distant isles, the immortality of the soul has always been, and still is, the belief of every people on the face of the earth. The knowledge of one God may have been obliterated ; his glory, power, and immensity may have been effaced, as I may say, from the hearts and minds of men; obstinate and savage nations may still live without worship, religion, or God in this world; but they all look forward to a future state. Nothing has ever been able to eradicate the opinion of the immortality of the soul; they

4

all figure to themselves a region which our souls shall inhabit after death ; and, in forgetting God, they have never discarded the idea of that provision for themselves."—[John-Baptist Massillon.]

Ah! me, what strange wild fancies crowd the brain
Of mortal man, who, wearied with the toil
And ceaseless combat of the rolling years,
Seeks rest in slumber deep and undisturbed.
His mind, transformed, becomes a temple filled
With forms intangible, immortal sprites,
From chaos rising, back to chaos borne.
Unnumbered throngs pass by, nor leave behind
A foot-print on the plains of memory.
But myriads, eager, clamor to be heard ;
And though the brain o'erwearied close the gate
And portals of the inner consciousness
To bar the phantoms out into the night,
Bolts cannot bar nor iron chain them down.
Returning swift with strength increased they knock
And thunder at the doorways of the soul
To gain admission, till they batter down
All barriers and rush triumphant in,
Bearing the captive Will in fetters bound.
The mind, unable longer to resist
Or strive for mastery o'er the spells they weave,
Follows submissive where their pleasure leads.
Lo! one of radiant form and face divine
There stood whose hands the Holy Bible clasped
Her brow, like fair Columbia's, broad and full,
'Neath which her brown eyes looked in wistful and
Intensely earnest tenderness, was bound
With fadeless wreaths of shining *immortelles ;*—
Not beauty, grandeur, and sublimity
Alone illumined and adorned her face ;
But mercy, purity, and perfect peace,
With deathless love harmoniously blent :—
As erst upon Mount Hermon, glory crowned,
Our Lord and Saviour Christ was round enwrapp'd
With shimmering mantle of supernal light,
Transfiguring His form and robes, until
His gleaming garments glittered white as snow,
And on His face the glow of lightning fixed,
While by Him Moses and Elijah stood :
So she in aureole of glory shone.
Oh! with what soul-ingulfing ecstasy
Rolled forth the story of her pilgrimage.

PHANTASMAGORIA.

Methought I stood within the court of Jove,
On high Olympus, where th' assembled gods
Extraordinary council held: for Jove,
Supreme upon his golden throne, had sent
His mandate by swift-winged Hermes forth
That all the gods within th' ambrosial vales
Of many-ridged Olympus should attend
To hear the Cloud-compeller's will declared.
His sister-wife beside him, white-armed Queen
Of Argos, Juno, sat; near by them sat
Their son, ferocious Mars, with wrinkled brows;
Pallas Minerva, blue-eyed goddess, shield
Of warriors, frowning on grim-visaged Mars,
Her sandals beautiful, ambrosial, bound
With golden bands unto her silver feet,
Beside earth-shaking Neptune proudly sat;
There Thetis, silver-footed queen, who sailed
Like swift-winged falcon from Olympus' heights,
"Charged with the glitt'ring arms by Vulcan wrought,"
For swift Achilles, Peleus' godlike son;
There Rhadamanthus, with the golden hair,
From far Elysian fields, stood near the gods;
Apollo, leaning on his silver bow,
Beside the laughter-loving Venus stood;
Here, hunchbacked Vulcan, skilled artificer;
There chaste Diana, hearth-stone guardian;
There Hebe, with innumerable nymphs
And lesser deities, all listening, wait.

Th' Olympian Temple, where the council sat,
Bore on its walls the trophies of renown
From ancient martial fields of gods and men:
Huge sabers, gleaming swords with golden hilts;
The massive, ponderous spear of Hercules
No human power could wield; th' elaborate shield
Which Vulcan wrought for Peleus' godlike son,
Upon whose golden disk were deftly graved
The scenes of peace and war; mysterious art!
A forge-wrought mirror of th' ethereal dome—
Metallic picture of terrestrial life—
Invulnerable armor 'gainst the foe—
The gleaming harbinger of Trojan doom.
When by the arrow sped from Paris' bow,
Upon the threshold of Apollo's fane,

Prostrate the chieftain, great Achilles, lay,
Ulysses strove with Ajax for the shield,
And won the prize: for though less strong of arm,
Yet wilier in council, he o'ercame
The craft of Ajax and bore off the shield.
Thence, burning with chagrin at his defeat,
Ajax rushed headlong into Hades' gloom.
Whereat the gods, enraged, a messenger
From high Olympus swift dispatched, to wrest
From mortal hands the golden armor wrought
By hands immortal. Thus the wondrous shield,
Whose stars the blood of noble Hector stained,
Was borne up to the temple of the gods.
Near by Achilles' armor hung the blade
Of King Leonidas, immortalized
By blood it drank at famed Thermopylæ.
Upon its hilt the *square and compass* flashed
In fiery light of costly diamonds set.
The brazen buckler called Ancile, dropped
By Mars, Rome's guardian deity, into
The hands of Numa as a shield against
The pestilence, and through the king's decree
Elev'n times copied by Mamurius,
Was here restored from Rome's decline and fall.
The shadow of the Twelve remains on earth,
In Numa's circle of revolving months.
Upon the left of Jove's imperial throne,
In sculpture wrought, I saw Laocoön
Writhe in the scaly serpent's hideous folds,
And in like torturing grasp, on either side,
His sons; their forms cramp'd by the tight'ning gripe,
Their visages transfixed with agony.
Above them, borne upon gigantic limbs,
High as the pillars of the Ephesian Dome,
The mammoth steed, by Pallas' art contrived,
In length and breadth like some vast oak-ribb'd ship
That o'er the billows of th' Atlantic rides,
Stood tow'ring like a frowning deity.
Immortal artists had adorned the walls
With speaking pictures of immortal powers.
Above the throne of Jove, by Vulcan wrought
In gold and silver, brass and glittering steel,
Emblems of Jupiter's almighty power,
Hung in relief, the execution of
Prometheus' sentence to Caucasian heights;

Immortal power brooked not that he should add
To mortal power of man the fire of art,
The pelf of forethought from Olympus filched.
And higher, reaching to the vaulted dome,
Great Saturn's overthrow, by which the gods
Won their immortal power through vanquishing
Their ancestor, offspring-devouring Time.
Great Alexander, on the eastern wall
In picture grasped a gleaming thunderbolt.
Upon the western wall Diana came
Returning laden from the prosp'rous chase;
While fronting Jove appeared historic scenes
Of combat on the plains of Illium,
And sage Ulysses' after wanderings.

The Cloud-compeller, from his golden throne,
In awe-imposing majesty uprose;
His golden breast-plate blazing like the sun,
A marvel to behold; in his right hand
The forked lightnings for a scepter grasped:
His glitt'ring throne creaked with his massive weight,
And underneath, the golden pavement shook
As if reverberating thunder sound:
Then the assembled gods he thus addressed:
"From that far distant, nameless orb, whence rolls
The great Jehovah's everlasting power,—
His who, alone, controls the destinies
Of all the gods that on Olympus dwell,
And sons of men that toil upon the earth—
Thence having just arrived, swift Iris, borne
Upon the wings of lightning, brings report
Of gath'ring hosts from all the circling worlds
That swing their cycles round Jehovah's throne.
Let all the gods in swiftest flight repair
Unto that nameless and far-distant orb,
And glean whate'er we may of destinies,
Foretold unto the swiftly gath'ring hosts
Now thither speeding from a myriad worlds.
Make ready all save Vulcan who alone
On Ida's topmost heights will keep strict ward
And watch o'er all th' Olympian boundaries.
But ere ye pass the portals of the Hours,
Let all the gods allegiant vows renew,
And, quaffing cups of sparkling nectar, pledge
Eternal fealty to immortal Jove."

CHORUS.

"Draw closer in th' Olympian ring—
Swear by the stars and by their King,
Swear by the dark infernal river
To keep thy plighted vow forever."

The waiting nymphs of Hebe bore to each,
A golden cup with sweetest nectar brimm'd ;
Then, drinking each to Saturn's mighty son,
Thus swore they all allegiance anew :
  "We swear to father Jove eternal love—
His mandate be our guide, his will our law."
The oath was sworn, and then the gods rushed each
A sky-traversing chariot to prepare.

First Pallas, child of ægis-bearing Jove,
Within her father's threshold drew her veil
Of airy texture, work of her own hands,
Across her brow, which towered above her eyes
Like rounded, snow-crowned mountain hanging o'er
Two deep-blue flashing lakes in vales beneath.
Her golden sandals, rich, ambrosial, spurned
The threshold ; o'er her snow-white shoulders flung,
Her streaming mantle like a comet blazed ;
And thus accoutered for her upward flight,
Her fiery car she mounted ; in her hand
A talisman caught from a thunderbolt
Hurled by her angry, cloud-compelling sire.
  With equal swiftness all the gods prepared.

The temple where th' Immortals sat in state,
The wonted clouds obscure from mortal gaze,
And when in thicker, darker folds are piled
The low'ring volumes on Olympus' heights,
Earth-plodding mortals fear Jove's wrath, swift to
Descend in lightning, tempest and in rain.
The grounds that from the temple's base extend
In gentle slopes far down the mountain's brow
Were interlaced with many chariot drives,
'Twixt which grew stately trees whose branches reached
The azure of the arching dome, and on
Their leaves, the stars like dew-drops twinkling played.
Grotesque, gigantic plants bloomed here and there,
Blood-sprinkled by Minerva till their deep
Carnation dyes mocked sunset's flaming hues ;

And from th' ambrosial nectar on them poured
By Hebe and her nymphs, their perfume breathed
Sweeter than odors from Hesperides.
Here, in the scarlet hyacinth, the blood
Of Ajax bloomed; and there, black roses from
Old Charon's garden on the murky Styx.
The birds of Paradise the verdure swept
With trailing plumage, sipping nectar from
These flowers of wondrous and unfading hues.
Among the bloom, white-armèd Juno's birds,
The gaudy peacocks, spread their brilliant plumes.
Swift-footed antelopes were bounding o'er
The lawns, and all the air was resonant
With warblings of the singing birds. I gazed
And listened in this garden of the gods,
While all their gorgeous chariots drew without
The portals guarded by the Hours; and then
I stood expectant and irresolute
Alone upon Olympus' airy heights,
In admiration gazing on the train.
As when some golden serpent, measureless,
Just breaking from the fetters of long sleep,
Unwinding its gigantic coils, its length
Majestic drawing out in swaying curves,
Marks out a trailing line of splendor by
Its aureate scales illumined by the sun;
So from th' Olympian gates the speeding gods,
In golden chariots through the azure wheeled
By their immortal coursers fleetly drawn,
Sailed in a train of splendor through the sky;
Great Jove the last, behind whose chariot streamed
A trailing quiver of white thunderbolts.

Scarce had he passed the portals of the Hours
When by my side a shining angel fell,
Who bidding me, Arise and conquer, said:
"Phantasmagoria, daughter of the West:
I come from those eternal palaces,
Where are assembled princes, potentates,
And dynasties from every earthly realm;
And whether now they live in history—
In this revolving temple of the living—
Or lie deep buried in oblivion,
Yet, far beyond yon gleaming sentinels,
That stand as watch-fires in the lower skies,

They hold accustomed espionage upon
Those realms where glittered erst their coronets.
When God in His eternal council sat,
On man's creation pondering, He called
Three ministers that wait about His throne
Responsive to his call, and to His will
Obedient—Justice, Truth, and Mercy; them
He thus addressed: 'Shall man created be?'
And Justice answered, 'Make him not, O, God,
For he will trample on thy holy laws.'
Truth answered, 'Make him not, O, God, for he
Thy hallowed sanctuaries shall pollute;'
But Mercy, dropping on her knees, exclaimed,
While looking upward through her falling tears,
'Make him, O God, and I will watch o'er him
With constant care, through all the darksome paths
That he may have to tread.' Then God made man
And said to him, 'O, man, thou art the child
Of Mercy; go and be thou merciful,'
Behold in me the angel Mercy, sent
To thee by Him whose love doth follow man
Round and around the earth, as ocean tides
Roll round careening to th' inconstant moon.
I come to tell thee that thou art ordained
To make a journey long and perilous;
That many deadly dangers shall obstruct
Thy way, and strange sights shall thine eyes behold.
Firm be thy faith and confidence in God,
And he will crown thy flight with victory.
I cannot be companion of thy course;
For I must keep my watch upon the earth,
While thou must seek the orb that far beyond
This mortal world, the universe of spheres
Concentric by its tensile radii holds.
As thou proceedest on thy way, thou shalt
Be guided by the light of other days.
The seers of ages past shall bear the torch
Of wisdom to illuminate the dark
Mysterious pathways of thy pilgrimage.
With faith in Christ, who died for men, be not
Afraid to conquer in Jehovah's name."
    Then I, as one that seeks for strength wherewith
To triumph over every danger, fell
Prostrate upon the earth, and cried aloud,
" O, Son of God, whose smile divine doth flood

With holy light the starry worlds that shine
And sparkle from afar, be Thou the guide
To light my footsteps from this earthly sphere
To shining realms of far celestial day.
Let golden showers at thy command,
Sparks flung from great Jehovah's hand,
Make luminous the blue ethereal dome,
And circling spheres around the Great White Throne."

Lo! a thick shining cloud upon me fell,
Born of Mnemosyne, from heights and vales
Of Helicon borne by swift-speeding winds,
Its magic heavy-laden depths with fleet
Returning memories teemed, with fragrant flowers
Of poetry, of choral dance, and song,
Of fertile fancies, eloquence and love.
But native to the heights and flow'ry vales
Of sunny Helicon, when to the high,
Cold, thinner air of Mount Olympus borne,
The magic mist was suddenly condensed ;—
Its elements became articulate ;—
The driving wind became twelve magic steeds ;—
The fertile fancies rolled four silv'ry wheels
Soft as the summer moonshine in the west ;—
The flow'ry garlands to a chariot turned
Which bore me onward in the train of gods ;
While for the viewless memories which ride
On rolling fancies of the laboring mind,
The Virgin Nine within the chariot rode,—
Great Jove's fair daughters by Mnemosyne :
Calliope, Muse of the classic brow ;
Then Clio, of the past, famed chronicler ;
Euterpe, sweet-voiced maid, with sounding shell ;
Melpomene, Muse of the tragic stage ;
Terpsichore, gay muse of twinkling feet ;
The love-lorn Erato, whose tender notes
E'er thrill with rapture earth-born maidens' breasts,
Who lit the torch of Hero to illume
The waves dark-rolling in the Hellespont,
When from Abydos bold Leander swam
To Sestos nightly, guided by her torch
Held o'er the deep, to woo him to her arms ;
Polymnia, sacred Muse, whose lofty strains
Roll praises toward the sky-enthroned stars,
Where the far-seeing Muse, Urania,

Marks out their orbits through the trackless void;
Last came Thalia, mirth-provoking Muse,
With quips and cranks, and laughter-wreathing wiles,
Who caught the reins of fancy in her hands,
To drive the fairy steeds upon the course
Marked out by wise Urania through the sky.
The winged steeds, swift as the flight of thought,
O'ertook Jove's thunder-trailing chariot,
And joined th' immortal sky-traversing train.

Now, ere the rolling chariot wheels had passed
Th' Olympian portals, Juno, white-arm'd queen,
Did challenge Pallas, blue-eyed goddess, to
A trial of their flying coursers' speed;
And that her own immortal steeds should first,
On bounding hoofs, the distant orb attain,
A cluster of her golden apples, from
The famed Hesperides, for wager laid
Against Minerva's dazzling sash, wov'n by
Th' adroitness of her own immortal hands
From out the golden fleece of Colchis, gemm'd
And broidered o'er with golden olives fair,
With massive clasp of gold, inlaid with pearl.
This wager blue-eyed Pallas did accept,
And called on all the gods to witness the
Immortal race 'twixt Juno and herself.

Entrancing scene! No mortal tongue could tell
The dazzling wonders which our flight revealed.
Far off I saw, with its Elysian bowers,
The famous garden of Hesperides,
Where crystal streams and flowing fountains spring;
Where loaded vineyards, orchards, beauteous vales,
And bounteous Terra's golden apple-trees.
A temple built of wine-tinged amethyst
To Bacchus 'mid the teeming vineyards rose.
The lofty walls were bathed in mellow hues,
That, blending, merged in softest harmony.
From open windows magic music flowed,
And hung entrancing in the fragrant air—
A siren voice in lays melodious sang
Of endless rest, of idleness, and ease.
Cool shades and grottoes, 'mid exotic bloom,
Exhaling Lethean odors on the air.
Delightful walk, sequestered nook, with rich,

Luxurious couch to tempt the weary limbs,
In lavish affluence 'round the temple lay.
Within the temple Bacchus reigns in state,
Where, 'mid unceasing revelry, his priests
On devotees and willing victims pour
Profuse libations of the ruby wine
In sacrificial worship of their god.
A statue of pure gold, to Mammon raised,
Stood central 'mid the golden apple-trees,
Colossal as the Sybynx of Egypt. In
The statue's hand a gleaming two-edged sword,
As mighty as the brand Excalibar
King Arthur wrested from the haunted mere.
They who would pluck the golden apples must
Submissive bow before the flashing sword.

Far upward, boundless, endless, and sublime,
The Milky Way stretched misty through the sky—
That thoroughfare where anciently the gods
Rode in their thundering chariots through the heavens;
Th' immortal coursers bounded on their way
Like long imprisoned warriors set free.
Inertia's viewless bands which bind unto
The ceaseless motion of the rolling earth,
The air, the clouds, and the swift-winged birds,
No longer held us in their ancient toils.
Earth's surface like a panorama passed
Beneath us, fast receding as it sped;
And in the curv'd arch of the azure east
Sank forests, mountains, lakes, and flowing streams.
The temples of the gods, half veiled in clouds,
On viewless chords suspended from on high,
Midway betwixt Olympus and the stars,
In long majestic curves vibrating swung,
As if in doubt whether to follow earth
Or like their tenants cleave unto the sky.
The temples, towers, and lofty monuments
By man's ambitious genius upreared,
Approaching the blue arch, seemed prostrate laid,
And, quiv'ring for a moment on the brink,
Sank headlong in the depths: while in the west,
From forth the curve that joined the earth and sky,
New forests, mountains, lakes, and flowing streams,
New cities, temples, towers, and domes uprose,
To pass like marshaled hosts in swift review.

Distance, soon o'er the fast-receding globe,
A rainbow colored mantle drew; then in
A shroud of cloud the land and sea were lost.

As through the crystal heights we sped, in that
Immortal race to reach the central orb,
In fragmentary song the Virgin Nine
Thus breathed the spirit of their favorite themes:

CALLIOPE.

As the moon sheds the light of the sun in the night,
    When rosy Eve covers him under the wave,
So the epic songs flame with the light of the fame
    Of heroes that sleep in the gloom of the grave.

CLIO.

While we ride through the æther liquescent,
    Let us sing, by the light of the stars,
Of the heroes whose fame efflorescent
    Shines forth through their manifold scars.

EUTERPE.

Our chariot is rolling along o'er the strings,
    To the lyre of the universe strung;
And the thrilling vibrations drop down from the wings
    Of the zephyrs in fragments of song.

TERPSICHORE.

The twinkling stars are dancing to the time
    Of harmonies now throbbing on our ears;
In rhyming orbits swinging to the chime
    Of symphonies vibrating through the spheres.

MELPOMENE.

The clouds before us like a curtain rise;
    The actors gather on the stage beyond;
The play shall be the nations' destinies;
    The hero, he who wields the conqueror's wand.

ERATO.

See how beautiful the moon's soft splendor
    On that tow'ring mount of low'ring cloud:
So shall tender love with soft touch render
    Bright the heart, erst lone and darkly proud.

POLYMNIA.

Earth-born passion, like the flash on
    Starry night by meteor hurled,
    Cannot light the darkling world

Through the gloom when doom shall crash on
  Crumbling spheres in chaos whirled.
Heavenly love, like fixed stars ever
  Blazing with unfading light—
In the darkness waning never—
Can alone illume the river
  Roaring to the realms of night.

URANIA.

The dome is like a charted scroll;
  I trace upon its face
The paths of myriad worlds that roll
  Through universal space.

THALIA.

My sisters sing in strains profound
Of all the universe around ;
Their favorite themes they all prolong
Until I weary of the song.
While flying from the cloudy earth,
Ring merry glees and songs of mirth.

PHANTASMAGORIA.

From these fragmentary shadows
Of the green and fertile meadows,
Where the feet of memory stray,
And untrammeled fancies play,
Which the muses from their singing
On the ambient air were flinging
Something of their inspiration,
Breathing of our destination,
  Dawned upon my wakening soul.
Then the mists of doubt that bound me,
In their breath dissolving 'round me,
  Cleared our pathway to the shining goal.

We swept far up the Milky Way, and saw
Great constellations and abysmal worlds ;
And stalking on their confines, phantoms gray,
Like mortal sentries to immortal ghouls
Transformed, doomed to eternal vigilance
Upon the ramparts of the rolling spheres.
Far as our gaze extended we beheld,
In number countless as the glitt'ring stars,
Swift-flying chariots speeding onward toward
The nameless and far distant orb, as if

The myriad worlds were sending heralds forth
T' attend the council ecumenical
Called by Supreme Omnipotence to sit
Within that distant central orb.   Far up
Above us, traversing the azure sky,
A flaming chariot rolled, drawn by twelve steeds
Of fire, on golden plumage swiftly borne,
Whose eyes, though full of woman's tenderness,
Yet with the valor of the lion flamed ;
Their shining manes streamed aft like flowing gold ;
Their hoofs of silver bounding on their way
Bright as the gleaming moons of Jupiter
In clangor echoed through the boundless air,
As echoed erst the dark-gray charger's hoofs
When, riderless from slain Mamilius,

> " Through many a startled hamlet
> Thundered his flying feet."

Bearing dismay to wounded Tusculum.
With nostrils wide distended, flashing eyes,
And speed of Jove's far-darting thunderbolts,
They marked a trail of splendor through the sky,
And from the chariot's circling wheels flashed showers
Of glimmering sparks, like falling stars dethroned.
Th' avenger of Mount Carmel rode within
Th' empyrean car, and, sitting by his side,
A *chieftain loved.*

His deeds—his worthy deeds alone—
Have rendered him immortal—
Eternal as the rolling sun,
That shines a thousand worlds upon,
And when the day of life is done
Illuminates Death's portal.

Resplendent round their forms
Played lambent flames, while twelve angels of light
Were hov'ring o'er the bounding fiery steeds,
And bands of cherubim and seraphim
On gorgeous floating clouds were marshaled by
The Archangel Azraël, attending hosts,
Upon the flaming chariot.

As erst
"The chariot of paternal Deity
Flashing thick flames," whereon the son of God,
"In sapphire throned," rolled on and headlong drove,
At great Jehovah's awful mandate, o'er

The crystal walls of heaven the angels who
Upreared the standard of rebellion : so
The radiant chariot of Elijah flew
Far through the crystalline empyrean.

Behind us far Achilles' radiant car
Came thund'ring, with the invulnerable chief,
And by his side the famed Patroclus rode.
Xanthus and Balius, the immortal steeds,
That erst, in mortal strife, thrice round the walls
Of Troy had dragged the fated Hector slain,
On bounding hoofs of hard cerulean steel,
Were swiftly clamb'ring up the ambient sky.
A princely pair behind the chariot rode,
The great Twin Brethren, who the Roman hosts
Led at the battle of Regillus Lake.

> "So like they were, no mortal
> Might one from other know :
> White as snow their armour was ;
> Their steeds were white as snow.

> "Never on earthly anvil
> Did such rare armour gleam ;
> And never did such gallant steeds
> Drink of an earthly stream."

Above us far the racing chariots
Of Juno and Minerva onward swept
In swiftest flight, by fleet steeds side by side
Drawn near and nearer to the distant goal.
Juno with whip of scorpions lashed her steeds
To pass blue-eyed Minerva's flying car ;
And Pallas plied the talisman, caught from
Jove's thunderbolt, her flying coursers' speed
To urge, Queen Juno's golden fruit to win.
While yet we watched their flight in matchless race,
Upon the way o'er which their chariots rolled,
The wandering Pleiad, lost from out the train,
Came swiftly rushing through the trackless void.
As when a blazing comet in its course
Doth threaten swift destruction to the orbs
Whose revolutions swing them in its path,
So did the wand'ring Pleiad menace now
The racing chariots of th' immortal gods.
The queen of Argos, stag-eyed Juno, quailed
Before the threat'ning orb, and fled the track

To let it pass. Not so Minerva, shield
Of warriors. On she sped and meanwhile prayed
"O, Father Jove, thy doubly daughter aid."
The Cloud compeller heard Tritonia's cries,
And hurling forward a swift thunderbolt,
Struck midway on its front the wand'ring orb,
Which cleft in twain let bold Minerva drive
Her flying steeds straight onward toward the goal.
The sky grew dark as with a gath'ring storm,
When, from its gloomy caverns, thunder-riv'n,
The orbless star sent forth with whirlwind sound
Legions of winged fiends, and giant birds,
Whose arrow-pointed plumage sped like darts,
Whose piercing howls, surpassing deep Hell's shrieks,
Thrilled through the darkened air to terrify
With horrid din the goddess in her flight ;
But scathless, nothing daunted, boldly rode
Minerva, whom nor thunderbolts, nor fiends
Thrice armed and winged with Terror's darts, could bruise.
Like some dark cyclone which at midnight sweeps
Destruction o'er a land or city doomed,
So did the breath of Pallas, blue-eyed queen,
Resistless as Niagara's strong flood,
All-grasping as Charybdis' howling whirl,
Send into Hades' gloomy depths the host
Infernal by Jove's thunderbolt released.
One vampire of colossal stature, huge
As Mars when prostrate by Minerva laid
On Illium's plains, sev'n acres covering,
Clung to her golden chariot with his claws,
And at the irate goddess taunting gibed.
She seized the hideous fiend, and poising him
High in the air, him headlong hurled against
The thunder-riven Pleiad's jagged rocks,
Whence swift rebounding, torn and mangled, down
He sunk into the gaping jaws of Hell.
Then Pallas, cheering her immortal steeds,
While from her scathless brow white thunderbolts
Glanced harmless, blazing round her awful form,
With gleaming splendor lumining the gorge,
Triumphant onward through the cleft orb swept ;
Then waved her golden sash above her head
To tantalize Queen Juno's envious eyes.
She, following far behind, in fury lashed
Her bounding steeds (as once in wrath she scourged

Diana, fair Latona's daughter, in
The battle of the gods, and made her flee
In terror to her father, Jupiter,
Upon th' Olympian Heights) now all on fire
To come ere Pallas, to the orb which lay
Beyond the dancing meteors of the night.

Like fleecy cloudlet driv'n before the blast,
Swift flying yonder sped the floating Isle
Of Delos, covered o'er with golden flowers,
Where first Apollo sprang to light of day,
And chaste Diana, Jove-begot, was born.
Saint Ursula there crowned with garlands fair
Of fadeless amaranth, fair Eden's bloom,
With virgin band eleven thousand strong,
All chanted praises in that hymn sublime
"O, all ye works of His, bless ye the Lord,
Praise Him and magnify Him evermore,
Ye angels of the Lord, bless ye the Lord,
Praise Him and magnify Him evermore."
That floating isle, where once Olympian gods
Reigned magnates in their undisputed sway,
Jove saw and sighed, as 'twere a picture of
The world wherein mythology had been
Subverted by the conquering faith in Christ.
Upon the coast rode Ursula's triremes,
Whose streaming pennons bore the Blood Red Cross;
Whose mariners divine commission bore
To sail the azure depths at will, alone
Subjected to Saint Ursula's behest.

Next far Alcyone, that distant orb
Which Maedler for the rolling universe
Fixed as the pivot, central, ultimate,
Round which all planetary spheres revolve,
Our gaze attracted. Nearer grown, and like
A blazing sun in volume now it seemed.
Great Jupiter beheld, and "Lo," he said:
"Yon sunbright sphere toward which our pathway tends!
Can that be Iris' distant central orb
Where reigns Jehovah on his awful throne,
And whither now from all the universe
The rolling chariots bear th' assembling throng?"
And as he spoke my eyes glanced searching o'er
The boundless plains and avenues of space,

Till in the shoreless sea of azure, sight
Was lost where finite joins the infinite.
E'en as I gazed Alcyone was passed,
And fast receding, dwindled to a star
Far in the traversed realms of space behind ;
So rapid now our swift increasing flight.
Still Jove seemed many things revolving in
His mind, and murmured of the Magi led
To Bethlehem when they had "seen His star."
Then turning he exclaimed, "Shall not that star
Which lit Jehovah's incarnation be
The scene for revelation of His great
Designs !"

      A sudden zone of darkness crossed
Our path, embracing races strange and worlds
Unknown. Here reining up our flying steeds
We paused. Below us far the glancing lights
Of ghostly cities twinkled. Giant shades
Colossal as the Cyclops walked the streets—
While yet we paused, the chariots of the Hours
Drawn by their rainbow-winged steeds swept by
Us like a whirlwind : Demogorgon sat
In one ; Promethens in another rode.

> "In each there stood a wild-eyed charioteer
> Urging the rainbow-winged courser's speed ;
> Their bright locks, streaming on ethereal gales,
> Trailed like a rushing comet's yellow hair."

Behind them, seated on his pale horse, Death
Rode from the darkened zone, in swift pursuit
After the rainbow-winged steeds that drew
The chariot of the Hours ; and henceforth like
A ghost his shadow hovered by our side.
Strange horrors seized me, waking fears appalled,
As multitudes of spirits 'round me thronged ;
Like withered leaves whirled by the autumn blast,
Their drifting forms in rustling robes rushed by
Driv'n by the viewless breath of Destiny,
Their voices echoing in the gloomy air :
Unearthly apparitions came and went ;
Ill-visaged, mocking demons shocked my sight,
And foul, insatiate harpies flapped their wings,
And with their blood-shot eyes, their horrid beaks
And crooked talons, menaced me. Teeth gnashed,
Flesh quivered, howling voices shrieked, until

I shrunk in terror from these hellish shades ;
" Then what is life ! " I cried in agony.
From out the darkness which around us rolled,
We heard the everlasting spirits cry.

FIRST SPIRIT.

The earth rolls ever 'mid the clouds ;
  Upon its face men grope in gloom ;
After spring garlands, snowy shrouds,
  After the bloom of youth, the tomb.

SECOND SPIRIT.

Life has two natures ; one that *seems*,
  Transient, like images ideal
Born on the fertile plains of dreams ;
  And one that *is*, unfading, real.
The life that *is*, springing from forth
  The radiance of light supernal,
Casts only on the cloudy earth
  A shadow of its form eternal.

THIRD SPIRIT.

Worlds unnumbered roll forever
  Through immeasurable space :
Though their axes shake and quiver,
  Clashing in their orbits never.
What unchanging, viewless trace,
Doth their swinging cycles render
Swerveless in their gleaming splendor !

FOURTH SPIRIT.

The chords of great Jehovah's love extend
  From His imperishable throne afar,
And to their everlasting orbits bend
  All worlds,—sun, satellite, and glittering star.
What beings people the remotest world,
  Bask in Jehovah's smile, pale at his frown,
And, when his wrathful banner is unfurled,
  Like withered leaves into the dust go down.

FIFTH SPIRIT.

Every planet has its angels
  Bearing to the wounded balm ;
After battle their evangels
  Whisper of the crown and palm.
Golden be their joys and treasures,
  Sunshine brighten every home,
Starlight gild each evening's pleasures,

While these orbs through ether roam;
For shall come a peal of woudrous
   Clangor, crashing ou the ears,
When Azrael sounds his thundrous
   Summons to the crumbling spheres.
In their orbits palsied, darkling,
   Universal worlds shall stand;
Quenched their gleaming and their sparkling
   By Jehovah's awful hand.

When over the desolate fields of the dead
Death's angels their hovering pinions shall spread,
The stars shall be wrapp'd like a corse in their shrouds,
And the universe sleep in its mantle of clouds.

SIXTH SPIRIT.

After darkness the reflection
   Of returning dawn upsprings;
After death, the resurrection,
   Flying on triumphant wings.

Lo! the blast of Gabriel pealing
Through Death's universe, unsealing
Bonds and fetters of th' unnumbered
Hosts that long in dust have slumbered.
Then the substance of Life's shadow,
Rising from each moor and meadow,
From beneath each bubbling fountain,
From the bleak and barren mountain,
From the once thronged, busy highway,
From each dark and lurking by-way,
From the forest and the lea,
From the desert and the sea,
Shall go forth, arrayed in vernal
Bloom and grace of life eternal.

Then over the fields of the waking dead
In triumph the feet of immortals shall tread;
And the stars all rekindled with immortal fire
Shall sweep in their course to a destiny higher.

SEVENTH SPIRIT.

The Earth rolls ransomed from its clouds;
   Upon its fields of shining green
Men, walking in transfigured shrouds,
   Reborn immaculate, are seen.
No dying groan, no widow's moan;

No clash of hostile spear or sword ;
The King of Kings is on His throne—
Our Saviour, Christ, the sov'reign Lord.

PHANTASMAGORIA.

Weary of the seen ideal—
Burning for the unseen real—
Yearning for the light to render
Visible the paths of splendor,
    Where the feet of Wisdom tread—
I will fly to yon bright mountain ;
I will drink of Faith's pure fountain ;
    By its inspiration led.
Through this glamour and delusion—
From this clamorous confusion
Let me gain the shining portals
To the realms of the immortals.

Worlds, cities, apparitions vanished all
Like wreaths of cloud merged in the darkened zone,
On depths below our vision fell, and in
The blackening profound, great Dante's Hell
Yawned low'rmost in the bottomless abyss.
Nine times around the murky vortex rolled
The sluggish Styx, while countless affluents
Branched through the measureless profound below.
Gray-bearded Charon in his ferry-boat
Upon the pitchy waves was ferrying
Innumerable throngs of lost and damn'd
From many worlds to Pluto's shady realms.
Upon the sombre portal's arch I saw
The immortal lines by Dante's genius carved :

> 'Through me you pass into the city of woe;
> Through me you pass into eternal pain ;
> Through me among the people lost for ay.
> Justice, the founder of my fabric, moved :
> To rear me was the task of power divine,
> Supremest wisdom, and primeval love.
> Before me things create were none, save things
> Eternal, and eternal I endure,
> All hope abandon ye who enter here.'

Close on the verge of Hell's confines, behold
"A fiery globe of angels on full sail
"Of wing;" the band that came and ministered
Unto our Saviour after Satan fled

From vainly tempting him upon the mount:
And now at Christ's command, around Hell's verge
They do forever wing their way, ablaze
With glory, in celestial harmonies
Praising the Father, Son, and Holy Ghost,
That Satan, hearing, may remember what
Is writ, "Thou shalt not tempt the Lord thy God."
The Cloud-compeller, gazing down the abyss,
Sought Satan, lord of Hell, upon his throne,
Which wrapt in densest smoke was hidden from
The immortal gaze of Jove's far-seeing eyes;
As if the arch-fiend some wily deep laid scheme
'Gainst mortal man and the immortal gods
Were plotting in the impenetrable gloom.
The brow of Jove then gathered in a frown,
And from his flaming red right hand he hurled
A thunderbolt down crashing through the depths
Of Satan's dark dominions, driving hence
The veil of cloud obscuring Satan's wiles,
And on his black throne laying bare to view
The reigning monarch of Hell's lurid realm.
The bolt crashed midway on the ebon throne
And lighted all the hollow of the vast
Recess, by its ten thousand fragments strewn.
Reclining like a huge leviathan
The thunderbolt disclosed the reigning fiend:
But startled by the sudden crash, he rose
And 'bove the apostate angels darkly towered
As Belus towered above the waters of
The Euphrates, or Gibraltar's fortress rock
Above the narrow sea that laves its base.
His fiendish legions by Beëlzebub
And Moloch marshaled, trembled as in dread
Before the flashing thunderbolt of Jove,
As trembled Pluto when the Ocean-god,
Earth-shaking Neptune, shook the boundless earth
And ocean wide.
Like dwellers in that orb most distant from
The sun—the fabled Apollonia—
Who far surpassed all children of the earth
In godlike beauty, godlike intellect,
In science, and in cultivated art;
Yet on their faces, ever fixed, the glare
Of painful, rayless, measureless despair.
                From Lucifer's black throne

Hell's flaunting banners waved, emblazoned with
The scene of many a conquest on their folds,
Won by the legions of Beëlzebub,
Triumphant on Hell's central banner glared
The loss of Paradise, where beauteous Eve,
In pristine loveliness, fresh from the mould
Of perfectness of feature and of form,
Reached forth to pluck and eat forbidden fruit;
The tempting serpent near with forked tongue,
With fixed, unwandering eyes, and ceaseless hiss,
Incarnate fiend, swung like a pendulum,
To sway and vibrate on the tree, and time
Man's fall—Death's introduction in the world.

As when the conflagration, that walks forth
In sootheless, raging fury to despoil
The doomed, devoted city, wraps his long,
Red, flame-fringed arms about the crackling walls,
The roofs, the lofty steeples and the domes,
In hot, fierce, eager, passionate embrace,
And to his blazing bosom madly holds
His yielding victim; gathering strength anew
From out the very whirlwind of his rage,
E'en Lucifer, convulsed with rage supreme
And horrid to behold, did wrathful grasp
The fractured thunderbolt down hurled by Jove,
And high above his triple-head, the fiend
Round and around the vivid lightning swung,
Until it glowed like Saturn's blazing rings,
Then hurled it back at cloud-compelling Jove,
Who, predivining Lucifer's intent,
Down simultaneous hurled a second bolt.
These meeting midway in the dark abyss,
Like mines exploded, lighting all the depths;
As when from old Vesuvius, belching flames
Illumed Pompeii's doom-night on the plains.
About the shield of Dis the lightning broke,
And all the plains of Hell made visible.

Behold, at intervals oäses fair,
And cooling springs, where fragrant flowers bloomed;
These were the footsteps of the crucified
Redeemer who "descended into Hell,"
Attended by th' archangels, Raphaël
And Michael, who, at His divine command,
In aftertime returning to Hell's depths,

Bore from the fiery flood the terrified
And weeping Margaret, while following
The tracks of Mephistopheles through all
The howling and the clattering of Hell,
In search of oath-bound Faust, eternal doomed
To wander ever in eternal woes.
Redeeming Love, omnipotent forbade
That her hell-luring, deathless love bereft
Of guardian angels and their care, should fix
Her doom in everlasting floods of flame.
The blazing eyes of lost, infernal hosts,
Like Tantalus, gazed longing on the bloom
Celestial springing from Plutonian plains
Wherever Christ and His archangels trod.
The cooling springs perpetual mocked their cracked
And parched throats, and forced infernal shrieks,
As they raged to and fro with madd'ning leaps
To break the fetters binding them to pain
Of fiery woe and quenchless thirst, in sight
Of cooling springs and fragrant vernal bloom.

Dis' brazen shield, round as the full-orbed moon,
Of massive weight and vast circumference,
Upon each field a Gorgon head engraved,
Colossal as the Sphynx and horrid to
Behold, encircled round by hellish charms,
Flashed in the thunder white, as flashed of old
God-like Achilles' shield when long-haired Greek
Rejoiced, and fated sons of Troy bewailed
Brave Hector, chief Priamides, laid low ;
For Dis, in dread of Jove's white thunderbolts,
Had grasped his ample shield to guard against
The wrathful Cloud-compeller's direful shafts.
From out th' abyss these echoes floated up,
Borne on the pinions of the Hell-born wind :
  "What to me are the evangels
    Of the white-winged singing angels
    On our revels shadows casting
    From their pinions everlasting ?
    What care I for the harmonic
    Grandeurs rolling in the tonic
      Chords of music round the Throne ?"

Thence leaving Satan 'mid th' infernal imps,
We onward sped to gain the distant orb,

Enveloped by impenetrable clouds,
Which Jove about us like a mantle threw.
Past suns and stars, through ether blue; past zones
Of brilliant asteroids, empurpled clouds,
Whereon great bands of angels rode and sung
The wondrous mysteries of the triune God ;
Past dancing meteors flashing through the night ;
Past sparkling planets with their silvery moons ;
Past blazing comets trailing crystal skies,
Until we reached an all-controlling sphere,
Where life wore beauty passingly sublime,
The one great center, energizing soul,
Inspiring, moving all created worlds.

O, orb supernal, where eternal dwell
Angels of light, make eloquent my tongue,
Thy glorious marvels worthily to tell.

Methought the very pinnacle was reached
Of all existence, whence all radiate lines
From that one universal center shot
Downward far through illimitable space,
Ethereal center of translucent sphere ;
That sphere the universe; and standing there
We gazed adown the radii, and saw,
In intertwining orbits circling round,
Millions of worlds harmoniously roll :
The sun hung in the doorways of the west
Pale as the moon. His borrowed radiance shed
No lustre on that native fount of light.

Juno and Pallas, with their panting steeds
And smoking chariots, waited our approach.
The golden apples which the goddess Earth,
From her famed garden in Hesperides,
Bestowed on Juno when she wedded Jove,
Adorned the breast-plate of Minerva's belt ;
For she had triumphed in th' immortal race.
Here all the gods reined in their steeds, which, loosed,
They bade upon ambrosial forage graze
Within celestial gardens fresh and green.
Then Jove, in glowing admiration o'er
The landscape gazing, said, this is, indeed,
Jehovah's golden "STAR of BETHLEHEM."

We trod upon a pavement of bright gold,
And mingled with a mighty throng that moved

With cadenced step along the golden street—
Adducent to a shining temple, far
Surpassing in its grand magnificence
All other temples, towers, and lofty domes.
Upon the temple's lofty walls was carved
In Hebrew character, embossed with fire,

" Lift up thy head and be thou strong in trust ;
For that which hither from the mortal world
Arriveth most be ripened in our beam."

Our onward march soon ,brought us to its doors.
I stood within its alabaster walls :
With fearful, trembling ecstasy I gazed
Around that mighty amphitheater.
My narrow vision scarce could grasp the maze
Of aisles and far-receding corridors.
The walls were lined with burnished diamond plates,
And on their face, in panoramic scenes,
Rolled pantomimic history of worlds.
A mellow lustre, native to the air,
Illumed the hollow of the vast recess,
And with imponderable touches lit
The alcoves, niches, and the arching dome,
The vaulted roof, sustained by golden piers,
Receding like the far-off canopy.
Was fretted o'er by scintillating gems,
Condensed and wrought from light original,
Whose glitt'ring shamed the stars that hang o'er earth,
As daylight doth a sickly taper's glare.
A massive chain, hung from the loftiest point,
Suspended an immense chronometer—
Timekeeper of eternity ! 'Twas called
THE WATCH OF AGES ! On its dial plate,
In characters of light unchangeable,
I read the seconds, minutes, hours, months, years,
And centuries, which far adown the dim
And shadowy vista of the past have rolled ;
The hollow spiral chain, link after link,
Showed Rome, Greece, Carthage and Assyria.
My utmost stretch of vision Eden reached :
What lay beyond a cloudy veil obscured.
Its mighty hands *remarked* the flight of time ;
Its pendulum with ceaseless motion swung,
As if hung up to time and regulate
The mighty enginery that animates

And wheels the planetary orbs throughout
The boundless realms of universal space.

Millions of people were assembled there,
In costumes common to all lands and climes;
Fair ladies sat beside gay cavaliers,
Displaying fashions of each century
Since first the myriad worlds began their march.
I heard all tongues that Babel's tower confused,
Yet comprehensible as household words;
All seemed to hear and understand them well,
And I, whatever were the words addressed,
Heard and responded in the self-same tongue.
My vision here ranged o'er th' unnumbered throng
Now gathered in the amphitheater.
There stood the Carthaginian Hannibal;
He leaned upon that blood-stained sword which waved
His legions o'er untraversed Alpine heights
Before Mount Calvary drank atoning blood;
There Alexander, who had wept because
No other worlds remained to be subdued;
And Khaled, merciless, whose Moslem blade
Converted full two hundred thousand souls.
Napoleon, the terror of the world,
Whose prison walls, while captive on the earth,
Did bound the arching canopy and lose
Themselves beyond the far horizon, stood
Encircled by his marshals and Old Guard.
Lycurgus, who was taught by Plato, and
Isocrates,—he who ordained the laws
Which gave to Sparta her immortal fame;
Pythagoras, who first the music of
The spheres proclaimed; Bozzaris with his band
Of Suliote warriors; Spartacus, the chief
Of gladiators; La Fayette, the friend
Of Freedom's temple risen in the West.
Cromwell was there, surrounded by a host
Of "Roundhead" followers; and Wellington,
Who conquered on the plains of Waterloo.
Moses, before whose rod the Red Sea waves
Were piled, as if in adamantine walls,
To let the sons of Israel pass through,
Ere refluent, ingulfing Pharoah's hosts.
David, the Hebrew shepherd, bard, and king;
Samson the strong, who on his shoulders bore

Alone the mighty gates of Gaza off;
And Solomon, the wisest king of eld,
Who reared the temple which the Son of God
Chose as the symbol of the corporate shrine
Of his incorporate Divinity.
There Sir John Franklin, who with reckless prow
Dashed 'mid the crystal, frozen, floating bergs
To find what flaming torches still relume
Th' Aurora Borealis in the North;
Confucius, Nathan, Solon, Socrates,
Justinian, Blackstone, Chitty, Story, Coke,
Prophets and seers of old-forgotten days,
With monarchs, heroes, warriors, and wise
Philosophers, and sages of all time,
Each by his satellites encircled round,
Sat watchful in that amphitheater.
Near by, with faces placid and serene,
Such as the brave and righteous ever wear,
The Signers of the Declaration stood;
And in their center, high enthroned in state,
Sat our immortal chieftain Washington!
Leonidas, the Spartan patriot king,
With band of heroes, who the Persian hosts
Of Xerxes fought at famed Thermopylæ.

> They fell devoted but undying;
> The very gale their names seemed sighing;
> The waters murmured of their name;
> The woods were peopled with their fame;
> The silent pillar, lone and grey,
> Claimed kindred with their sacred clay;
> Their spirits wrapp'd the dusky mountain;
> Their memory sparkled o'er the fountain;
> The meanest rill, the mightiest river,
> Rolled mingling with their fame forever.

Beside the Spartan band and with them one
In fellowship of glory, stood the band
Whose blood made Balaklava holy ground.

> Stormed at with shot and shell
> Boldly they rode and well;
> Into the jaws of death,
> Into the mouth of hell
> Rode the six hundred.

In light of newer advent, but immersed
With them in baptism of fraternal death,—

Kindred with them in forlorn valor, stood
The martyred few who with brave Custer fell.

Near by in light of ancient splendor stood
Godlike Achilles with his Myrmidons,
And glorions Hector, patriot chief of Troy,
And by his side the fair Andromache ;
There Argive Helen, by her primal lord,
The valiant Menelaüs stood redeemed ;
I turned to where great Dante stood, and asked
What meant this host assembled from all climes ?
Was this the temple of the gathered dead ?
Did high and low, the evil and the good,
Here mingle in eternal blessedness ?
" It cannot be the universe of Hell ;
For but e'en now, in flight with all the gods
Upon the Muses' flowery chariot borne
From high Olympus, I beheld far down
Below the Milky Way on which did bound
Th' immortal steeds, the murky orb on fire.
It cannot be thy Purgatory, for
Nowhere do I behold the Trinal steps,
With rock of flashing diamond bright, whereon
God's angel stood to guard the port which led
Unto the Rocky Way. It cannot be
Thy Paradise, for lo, thy Muse hath sung

> None ever hath ascended to that realm,
> Who hath not a believer been in Christ,
> Either before or after the blest limbs
> Were nailed upon the wood.

And some, I know,
Assembled here own not Messiah's name.
Then Dante in a voice of love replied :
"I seek a mount called Faith, whose summit shines
In the clear atmosphere of truth above
The clonds perpetually rolled in dark
Obscuring volumes of high-colored wiles
About its base, where wrestling mortals strive
In Life's fierce battle on the dusky plains.
Born in the region of diviner light
Than gleams from pageantry of thronèd kings ;
Loyal alone to the imperial sway
Of Progress in the Right, monarch august,
Before the thunder of whose conquering tread

The ancient realms of darkness, crumbling fall.
Eager to speed his onward march, and ban
The rolling volumes of delusive wiles
That hide the mount of Faith, I stand and gaze
Upon the mirrored life of centuries;
And while I gaze, from out the wreck-strewn depths
I hear the voices of the ages speak:"
'In every empire of the world, the gems
Clasped in the gold of royal diadems—
　Set there by stolid craft of Prejudice,
Designed in Error's gloomy studio,
And cut in light of Passion's lurid glow—
　Are tarnished with the blood of Sacrifice.'

Then I to Dante said: "O, bard sublime! how may I arise and conquer? What shall the armor be?" And he, answering: "What shall the armor be? *Truth;* truth in thought, in speech, in action; truth to duty, to your fellows, yourself, and your God. The more nearly you approach to absolute truth the more nearly you will approach to absolute perfection. The end of learning is knowledge of truth, and the use of knowledge is excellence of action.

　　'If I were a voice, an immortal voice
　　　That could travel the wide world through,
　　I would fly on the wings of the morning light
　　And speak to men with a gentle might
　　And tell them to be true.'

"If truth in man is a gem of great price, truth in woman is a gem above all price and the chief jewel of her crown."

Then Dante Alighieri led me forth
That I might view the wondrous works of art
Which all the temple's alcoves did adorn.
I joined the sapient train and onward moved
Through countless myriads congregated there
Until we reached the vast and glittering throne
Whereon immortal Shakspeare ever reigns.
Half hid in shining clouds Melpomene
Above the monarch hovered, scattering flowers
Whose perfume fell in torrents round his head.
Upon the panels of the eight-sided base
Whereon the throne was reared, Pygmalion
With his life-giving chisel had engraved
The living forms of Hamlet and King Lear,
Othello, Desdemona, and Macbeth,
Coriolanus, Shylock, Richard Third,
The Merry Wives of Windsor, Cymbeline,

The Royal Henrys, Falstaff, and King John,
Great Julius Cæsar, Brutus, Antony,
Midsummer Night's Dream's phantasies grotesque,
And Romeo, by the viewless cords of love,
Set with the seal of Death, to Juliet bound,
By the divine afflatus all relumed
With life and beauty, sentience, and strength,
They seemed, like sentries incorruptible
Standing upon the ramparts of his realm
To hold the ages to allegiance.

Proud monarch of the drama! In thy verse
Hath every phase of human passion found
A voice and eloquence of utterance.

There stood Cervantes, with the laurel crowned,
Token of his victorious crusade
Against the wind-mill giant—"Chivalry."
The youthful, austere Chatterton beside
Him reveled in the marvels of antique
Creations in the theater displayed,
Which neither high-born Walpole's cold distrust
Nor unrelenting poverty could blast ;
Only immortal genius like his own
Such grand immortal harmony could grasp.
Goldsmith and Gray were talking of the scenes
That won from each the thrilling voice of song ;
In the "Deserted Village" one breathed out
A tender reminiscence of the past.
From vacant rooms the tenants had gone forth
And only left a shadow of their forms,
Only a lingering echo of their tread
To prompt the poet's singing memories ;
But in their graves they found a deathless fame
In the sweet-flowing "Elegy" of Gray.
Racine and Corneille, of dramatic fame,
Were listening to some strangely wrought conceit
Of Goethe's wild imagination born.
Poe stood with melancholy face alone,
As if from off the bust of Pallas, still
He heard the black-plumed raven's "Nevermore."
The sweet-voiced Moore almost with envy heard
The wandering Exile's footsteps on the beach ;
For Campbell's reaching Fancy had plucked forth
From Erin's Isle the choicest fruits of song.
Clay, Sumner, Webster, Thomas, and Calhoun
3 DO

Round Stonewall Jackson and McPherson stood,
Discussing all Ambition's burning thirst,
Which only draughts of crimson blood can quench.

While Hawthorne listened to the bards' discourse,
Over against the Temple's eastern front
Through the dissolving mist, Benevolence
Beamed suddenly from forth the "GREAT STONE FACE!"
Beholding, all grew still,—inly convinced
That though they had the gift of prophecy,
And though they had all knowledge and all faith,
So that they could remove the mountains hence,
And had not charity, then they were nought.

As from his throne the monarch Shakspeare gazed
Upon the kindred bards that crowned him king,
Bending to listen to their speech, anon
Enriching by some aptly spoken word
Th' elaboration of their varied themes,
The Hebrew shepherd, bard and king approached.
Instinctively the reverent throng apart
Divided, that the Psalmist might pass through.
In Shakspeare's hand he placed the palm and crowned
Him with the laurel wreath. Then they conversed
Of Hebrew art, philosophy and song,
And of the myriad bards unknown to fame
(Since rose the Temple of Jerusalem)
Whose "Footprints on the sands of time" have left
The impress of the spirit of their age.
A wistful look of earnest interest
Upon the old King's royal visage beamed,
While Shakspeare thus the train of thought pursued:
"As by the fossil fauna late exhumed,
Or imprint of the palm or fern upon
Th' enduring rock, the skilled expert discerns
The climate and the kindred products of
Their sev'ral eras; so may we discern
From the still living fragments of old song
The spirit and the temper of the times.
When they were breathed, though millenary dust
Obscure the name and fame of them that breathed.
Thus shall the "Song of Hiawatha" show
To future ages the primeval race,
Though then extinct, which erst untutored roamed
Through pathless wildernesses in the west;
So shall the desolating tread of caste

On 'Aylmer's Field,' when progress shall have poured
Its Lethean billows on the pride of birth,
Raise from the dust the moldering skeleton
Of pompous rank by feudal bondage won.

The golden fancies and the pure, chaste style
That mark their verse, illumined by the fire
Of noble impulse blazing in its flow,
Have won for Longfellow and Tennyson,
Within the realm of the immortal bards,
A crown of honor and a robe of light
Which, for their advent, with a welcome wait."

As Shakspeare closed, the bards approving all,
Near by them Paganini woke the soul
Of melody in the sweet "Song of Gold."

In company with the sapient train
I onward mov'd enraptured by the scenes.
We passed by Aristotle, Socrates;
By Romulus and Remus, the twin-sons
Of Rhea Sylvia, by Mars begot;
By Alcibiades, Herodotus,
Demosthenes, Mazzini and Plutarch;
By Plato, Æsop, old philosophers,
Ancient historians and orators;
And the more modern sages, Audubon,
Agassiz, Franklin; and a thousand kings
And potentates whose fame the bards have sung.
Here Socrates and Plato held converse
Upon the wondrous beauty, majesty,
And fadeless scenes upon the burnished walls
Within the Theater of the Universe;
Then of that changeless law which holds its seat
In great Jehovah's bosom, and whose voice
Rings in the harmony that moves the world.
Here solitary walked great Constantine,
Th' imperial monarch, whose ambition gave
First legal basis to the Church of Rome;
There, Henry, son of Richmond, panoplied
In vestments of Pontific dignity
Usurped, stood as a monument of strength
Unbridled, and of passion unsubdued,—
Founder of English Catholicity:
Elizabeth, his daughter both by blood
And native character, beside him stood;
Near by, the cultured, beautiful, serene,

But fated Lady Jane, nine days a queen;
The giant Luther, great iconoclast,
By birth a rustic, but in strength a king,
Of dauntless valor and unbending will:
Ægisthus and false Clytemnestra, pale
And haggard, wandered still pursued
And haunted by Tisiphone, the blood
Avenger of King Agamemnon's death.
We reached the Temple of Fame, a monument
To Pope who wrought into a golden tongue
Great Homer's Iliad and Odyssey.
"The Eastern front was glorious to behold
With diamond flaming and barbaric gold."
Here Homer paused before these tributes, mute,
Paid by a modern bard to ancient song.
Clear flashed those scenes before the poets' gaze
By whom rehearsed long centuries ago:
As when to Dido's halls, Æneas came
A wandering fugitive from vanquished Troy,
Tossed on tempestuous seas by hostile winds,
And in her picture galleries beheld
Himself and comrades reproduced, and saw
Again the walls of Troy o'erturned, himself
Escaping, Hector slain, Creusa lost,
By Libyan artist vividly portrayed.

   Within the Temple of Fame, assembled throngs,
In rapt attention, gazed upon a stage
Where Kean, Macready and the elder Booth,
And many celebrated actors from
All ages and all climes, portrayed
The tragedy of Maximilian's fate.
I saw Europia's kings, from many of
Whose veins the blood of Maximilian flowed,
Intently gazing on the tragedy.
I heard the player in the Emperor's role
Soliloquize upon the omens thus:
"The lurid sky glowers ominous above,
As if the sun in anger frowned upon
The throne where erst his worshipers alone
Held sway: ere Cortez, with his armored few,
Forced with the sword, upon the Aztec realm,
The first faint glimm'rings of the source whence springs
The light which Montezuma worshiped in
The sun, nor knew of other source beyond.

Along the snowy Cordilleras' heights,
I see the fires of revolution glow:
Juarez with his Aztecs offers up
Oblations on their altars to the sun.
O! thou eternal God, great source of light,
Who didst th' anointed anciently endow
With grace, with wisdom, and with sovereign power,
Endow me with the wisdom to reign o'er
This wasted realm, by anarchy distraught;
Or if the royal blood of Europe be
Not meet for the redemption of the state,
Grant that its sacrificial flow appease
The rage and desolation of revolt,
And bring the land of my adoption peace."
The next scene brought the melancholy rôle
Of the depressed Carlotta, seeing with
Prophetic vision harbingers of woe;
I heard the player of the rôle thus speak:
"I cannot of its fears my mind divest,
Nor penetrate the gloom that gathers round.
Last night as I in slumber dreaming lay,
I saw the body of the Emperor
Encoffined; and I heard the people shout—
Oh! HOW *they shouted!* 'He is murdered'—
Oh! coward heart, be still thy throbbing—*hark!*
What sound is that which breaks upon the night,
As if the very air were cracked and crumbling?
Strange horrors now appall me, and I know
Not what to do or whither I must fly.
If there be fluids, as we know there are,
Which, conscious of the dreadful coming storm,
In their glass arteries shrink up, and strive
To hide themselves, may not the blood as well
Be conscious of the thirsty, unseen hand
That comes to let it flow, and in that hour
With icy coldness, back recede, and knock
For entrance at the doorways of the heart?
'There is a tide in the affairs of men
Which, taken at the flood, leads on to fortune,'
So Marcus Brutus said upon that night
Wherein his evil spirit did appear.
The flood of which he spake bore him unto
But bitter fortune on the bloody plains
Of Philippi. Perhaps the flooding tide
Whereon *he* is afloat may sweep *him* to

'That bourne from which no traveler returns.'
Hark! pealing, dirge-like, o'er the dark blue wave
The midnight bells are tolling for the brave:
Oh! God, 'tis done, my aching heart knows well,
Too well, the doom these throbbing pæans tell:
Black billows of despair upon me roll—
Affrighted reason quits my frantic soul."

   *   *   *   *   *

A sudden peal rang on the startled ear—
The WATCH of AGES tolled a nation's knell.
Then Dante Alighieri gazing in
The mist of ages gone, like one who sees,
As in a vision, suffering and sin,
Thus painted Desolation's cruel reign :
  " The powers of earth are subject to decay ;
They have their birth, their growth, their life and death.
As forest oaks are nourished by the mold
Of trees ancestral, perished and decayed,
So from the dust of crumbling empires spring
New empires, flourishing in strength of youth
Until imperial glory's noon is reached ;
Then, at the heart corrupt, unseen decline
Begins, and gnaws with silent teeth, until,
Outspreading, but a hollow shell remains ;
When, as the oak whose days are numbered, rent
From its foundation by the tempest's breath,
Down, crashing 'mid the tender saplings, reels,
And scathes or crushes many in its fall,
So falls decaying empire's hollow shell ;
And growing States, its shadow underneath,
Are startled at the sound.   While some are bruised,
And some are crushed beneath the cumbrous weight,
Yet others send forth roots to pierce the mold,
And thrive upon the fallen state's decay.
Thus life is ever feeding upon death.
  The length of days allotted to the tree
Of liberty is as the strength with which
Its roots are fixed within the people's hearts,
And as corruption's gnawing fangs are banned
From its own heart; as it is pruned
Of cumbrous branches and of surplus growth ;
As cultured by untiring industry ;
As warmed by sunbeams of intelligence,
And watered from the springs of charity.
Valor and Love should wed; their offspring, Faith

And Virtue, should be crowned with knowledge, and
Endowed as guardians of Liberty.
　Until the dawning of millennial morn ;
While sin and passion throng the human heart ;
While greedy av'rice feeds on poverty ;
While mad ambition drives his brazen car,
Without remorse, o'er meek humility ;
While lost, in conquest, honest love outspeeds ;
While truth is fiction, falsehood, current coin ;
While might makes right, and wrong in law is mailed ;
While folly lures, and wisdom drives away ;
While a great name is the ideal god,
And the Great God but an ideal name,
Shall mortal be the Tree of Liberty."
　The voice of Dante died upon the ear
As dies an ocean of rich melody,
When waves of sound receding in the mist
Are further—further borne away, till naught
But echoes answering from the distant hills
Vibrate declining in the eager ears ;
Yet when the waves of sound have ceased, within
The chambers of the soul, their sweetness still,
Like some fond ling'ring spirit, waits to sing.

　Now turning from the Temple we passed on
To where famed Æschylus and Shelley 'tranced
Th' Olympian gods with passages and scenes
From the "Unbound Prometheus," while we paused
To gaze upon the scene, the glance of Jove
Standing supreme among th' Olympian gods,
On Homer fell ; "Behold," he said, "the scribe
Whose record teems with our immortal fame—
His own imperishable monument.
Though to his sightless eyes Aurora brought
No radiance upspringing in the East,
Yet through the open windows of his soul
Calliope flew with her flaming torch
To guide the flight of his immortal song.
Green be th' ambrosial fields where walk his feet—
Fadeless the aureola round his brow."
Then fairer forms and faces gazed we on
Where Joan of Arc and Sappho, the Tenth Muse,
Clothed in celestial robes conversing walked.
The Maid of Orleans, from her wings of flame,
On which she flew to immortality,

Drew forth a fiery plume which Sappho took
To write in burning words the infamy
Of Warwick and Beauvais. Matrons and maids
Whose names shine forth like stars in history
Around them thronged; Evangeline, the fair
Acadian maid, whose wandering feet pursued
Lost Gabriel no more; fond Josephine,
The haughty monarch's loving bride cast off
At *his* resistless ruler's rude behest—
Volting Ambition's voice; Roman Lucrece;
Virginia; the beauteous Capulet,
Whose heart o'erleaped hereditary hate,
Obedient to the thrilling voice of Love;
Fair Isabella, queen of proud Castile
Who sacrificed her royal jewels on
The altar of Spanish marine research.
And Beatrice, Dante's youthful bride,
Wearing a crown immortal.

                    Passing thence,
Vast multitudes in endless trains moved on,
As if illimitable ages gone
Were passing in review their heritors.
I saw Lorenzo, the magnificent;
And Tycho Brahe with Galileo
In converse on the rolling of the spheres.
The author of the "Christmas Carols" walked
With Burns, the Highlanders' beloved bard;
Firdousa, famed bard of the Orient;
Josephus, who transcribed his people's woes
In pay and interest of their conquerors;
Albert, Victoria's well-beloved prince,
With Nelson, Perry, Farragut, and Foote;
The daring Cushing, bravest of the brave;
Mahomet, founder of the Moslem faith,
With Bunyan, Sophocles, and Rabelais
The doctrines of the Koran canvassing;
Cassandra, too, with burning eloquence,
Portrayed to Lope de Vega the chagrin,
The pain, the sorrow of the fatal gift
Of prophecy unhonored, and of fate
Revealed, but unbelieved. She cried aloud:
"Alas! they little knew the scenes of woe
That oft had made a fountain of mine eyes.
Their ears had never drunk the piercing shrieks

That to my ears forever had untuned
The melody of hearthstone rhapsodies.
Their dreams had never pictured agonies
Which I had seen, and heard, and felt, and known.
The murderers of Agamemnon oft
Stand round me with their gibing taunts, as, when
Before the altar I became his bride,
I saw him seated at the banquet board
Amid his guests, and standing o'er them their
Assassins, ready for his victim each.
With fiendish malice, ever and anon,
They stop and glare, with horrid mien, at me.
Great God! I see them now; their red eyes glow
Like meteors in the canopy of hell;
Their breath is colder than boreal gales
Which sweep at midnight from the Arctic zone.
As died the accents of the Prophetess,
Behold, two stately and majestic forms
Walked arm in arm in earnest converse rapt.
One had unfolded a new world to view,
Sailing against a superstitious tide
Of ignorance into the unknown west.
The guerdon his ungrateful sovereign gave
Was ward and fetters in the dungeon's gloom.
The other in the might and majesty
Of sterling manhood on the New World's soil
The tree of Liberty had planted and
Matured against the pride, the opulence
And valor of Europia's chivalry:
Though born a slave, yet monarch in the sway
He bore o'er passion, prejudice and caste,
He won the richest province owned by France
From wasting anarchy and foreign foes,
And held it for th' imperial sovereign.
That sovereign's guerdon was starvation in
A dungeon.
      O! Columbia, hide thy face
While the inventor and the savior of
Thy verdant sister in the sunny seas
Pass in their glory by.
            When Ferdinand
And great Napoleon by the Lethean waves
Of Time and Progress shall be overwhelmed,
Their fame declining into infamy,
The names of Christopher Columbus and

Of Toussaint L'Ouverture shall live enshrined
Within the hearts of Freedom's champions.

While yet I stood with soul absorbed in all
I saw, great Dante cried, " Look thou upon
The holy scenes that flash in splendor o'er
Yon glitt'ring walls ; there do the oracles
Of God reveal what man is fain to know."

Like quivering moonbeams on a glassy sea,
Or like the vivid lightning through rent clouds,
Before the dreadful thunder's crash and roll,
Immortal pictures flashed out on the scene.
Had I the wealth of Dante's great conceit,
Far-reaching to the bounds of mortal ken ;
Or tongue or pen whose eloquence surpassed
Immortal Homer's rhapsodies, yet could
I neither worthily conceive the scenes,
Nor aptly utter or portray the gleams
Historic and prophetic playing o'er,
And flashing from the burnished diamond plates.

Here belched a thund'rous battle of the gods ;
There, fleeing phantoms, sped the wand'ring Jew ;
Where desolation swept the checkered scene
Wept Zion's daughter o'er Jerusalem.
Here bending o'er her first-born, mother-love
With face irradiate, mantled o'er by flush
Of joy, or settling in serene content ;
There meek-eyed Charity withdrew the veil,
Disclosing Christ and her whom none condemned,
Bade by her Saviour " Go and sin no more ;"
Here Jupiter with roses crowned, from high
Olympus, drove the railing Momus forth ;
There Æsop through the shadowy forest roamed,
In converse with all nature animate ;
The prophet Daniel, glory-crowned, whose faith
Stamped calm serenity upon his brow,
Whose godlike gaze, and heart with strings of steel
O'erawed the raging lions in their den,
And paralyzed their fanged but pulseless jaws ;
There the Madonna Di Foligno, wrought
By Raphael of Urbino ;—not the thin
And unsubstantial canvas, deftly swept
By mortal touch, with fading earthly hues,
And only shadowy semblance of relief,

As borne upon the walls of Vatican;
For earth-bound art vouchsafed to Raphaël
But murky reflex of conceptions grand
Of his immortal genius begot;
But in the walls of this theatric hall,
Where execution might keep pace with thought,
Th' untrammeled hand of Raphael had eclipsed
Conception with the grace, the life, the breath,
The wondrous mingling of Divinity
With virgin purity and mother-love,
Transfiguring Madonna perfected;
Here the Archangel Michael vanquishing
The Lord of Hell; there Ananias led
To death with false Sapphira; Moloch drunk
Upon the plains of Tophet with the blood
Of Innocents, by Herod's harsh decree
Destroyed; the deluge overwhelming all
The world, through Heaven's opened windows down
By wrathful hand of great Jehovah poured:
Swift following came Leonardo's grand
Depiction of a Saviour's sacrifice;
Christ on the verge of death, surrounded by
His followers who ate and drank his blood
And body; fixed amazement sat upon
Their visages, while on his face serene
Calm resignation settled like a dove.
Wondrous twin pictures of Divinity !
Wrathful Jehovah drowning sin from earth,
And merciful Messiah saving man
From everlasting penalty of sin.
Then came the garden of Gethsemane:
The blood-red moon hung in the angry sky,
Betokening the morrow's bloody deeds.
To lurid heavens the Saviour raised his eyes
In agony of prayer. Great drops of blood
Oozed from his pallid face, while bending low
Beseeching that the cup of bitterness
Might pass, yet bowing to the Father's will.
Near by, Jerusalem with spires of gold,
The Fortress of Antonio upon
The rock beside the temple stood; within
Was Pontius Pilate's judgment hall.
Upon Mount Zion, on the other side,
The palace of the Tetrarch Herod stood;
And thither, 'mid a clamoring multitude,

Was Jesus borne for Herod to pronounce
Upon His guilt or innocence; then crowned
With thorns, and clothed in purple robes, with jeers
And mockings and revilings, He was led
Back to the court of Pilate for decree,
And Pilate wrote in Hebrew, Latin, Greek,
This accusation for the crucifix,—

"IESVS NAZARENVS REX IVDÆORVM."

That vision passed, and lo! a sad-voiced train
Of singing pilgrims, breathing forth in strains,
As 'twere a well-tuned harp of sweet accord
Struck by the hand of grief, and quivering
Responsive to the spirit of the touch.
I listened with intensest eagerness,
And "*Miserere mei Deus*" heard
With strangely sweet, though sad, vibrations rise
Funebrious on the sympathetic air.

   *   *   *   *   *   *

As faded into air the lingering strains,
The crucifixion came swift-following,
And sudden darkness settled like a pall;—
As if the Holy Ghost, God's Robe of Light
Ineffable, in rayless, spotless folds
Lay waiting to enshroud him for the tomb.
Terrific earthquakes shook the blackened night;
The cleft rocks groaned with harshly grating sound;
Graves yawned, and from their hollow depths the dead
Walked forth in phosphorescent garments clad;
Horrific apparitions! man in form—
In substance only shining, spectral shades.
Thick gloom, despair, and blackest darkness reigned.
Then came the rent tomb, whence emergent walked
A risen and immortal God, in light
Unspeakable, and full of glory bathed.

The changing scenes brought next before our view
That grand and terribly magnificent
Portrayal of the final Judgment Day
By Michael Angelo, translated and
Transfigured. On the Great White Throne Christ sat,
And judged the world, by angels round engirt.
The seven angels with sev'n trumpets stood,
There on the left the fallen and the lost
Inheritors of deep damnation and

Of untried woes: Grief, terror, and despair
Froze on each visage like the ice of death.
Here were the rent rocks, there the opening graves,
And Minos passing sentence on the damned.

O! genius, that grasped the rainbow tints
And framed them into great Jehovah's praise.
  Swift-coming pictures, countless as the stars
Of heaven, played upon the burnished walls.
Celestial visions! how ye fled my grasp
Of touch and sight, as flitting sunbeams pass,
And only left a sparkle and a glint
Of your supernal glory darkling in
The lonely chambers of my memory!

  Amazed, bewildered, and perplexed by all
I saw and heard, I turned once more and sought
From Dante inspirations crowning light.
"Behold," he said, "The Play of Destiny!"
  Methought that Handel's grand Messiah rose,
And, like an ocean of rich melody,
In swelling billows of sweet concord rolled
Throughout the amphitheater's vast nave.
The curtain rose, and on the stage a choir
Of myriad white-winged angels stood.
A waving veil of shining vapor hung
Beyond the choir, translucent, liquid, through
Whose folds supernal light unceasing streamed,
And trenchant seraphim unrippling passed,
Careening in the light, the vap'rous veil
Exhaled harmonious hues responsive to
The concord of the oratorio
And pealing from ten thousand choristers,
Enrapturing alike the eye and ear,
As all the angels and archangels sang:

"Lift up your heads, O ye gates, and be ye lift up ye everlasting doors, and the
King of Glory shall come in.
  Who is the King of Glory?
  The Lord strong and mighty: the Lord mighty in battle.
  Lift up your heads, O ye gates, and be ye lift up ye everlasting doors, and the
King of glory shall come in.
  Who is the King of Glory?
  The Lord of hosts; He is the King of Glory.

Chorus.

"Hallelujah! for the Lord God Omnipotent reigneth.
  The kingdom of this world has become the kingdom of our Lord, and of His
Christ; and He shall reign forever and ever;
  King of kings, and Lord of lords; Hallelujah!"

As past in softest melody the last
Expiring note of that triumphal hymn,
The waving vap'rous veil dissolved, and lo!
A city of surpassing splendor lay
Before us, with its spires and pinnacles
All specked with gold; and flashing in the beams
Of supernatural light, uplifted high,
Shone many a cross of gold, that spoke
Of temples dedicated there to God.
The Rock of Ages in the city stood;
Upon the Rock of Ages founded, rose
A temple vast, transparent, strong, secure—
TEMPLE OF TRUTH, 'twas called—old as the cross
On Calvary's heights.

          Diana's Temple built
At Ephesus, a tribute from the hearths
And homes, the willing hearts and ready hands
Devoted to the goddess chaste, whose ward
Preserved home altars 'gainst marauding lust;
Ionic columns, Parian marble jets,
Green jasper walls, cut and embellished by
Etruscan, Doric, and Romanic art,
Where Mongols, Greeks, and Romans sacrificed
In worship of their favorite deity;
     Saint Peter's Church at Rome, most ancient and
Magnificent cathedral, reared above
The hallowed ground where, moldering, repose
The sacred ashes of the martyred saint.
Four score and ten years from the Saviour's birth
The Bishop Anacletus memorized
The spot of his great predecessor's tomb
By building up an oratory there.
Two centuries more and sixteen years passed by
And Constantine, the Roman Emperor,
Built a basilica above the tomb.
When other gliding centuries had lapsed,
The modern masters of Italian art
Upreared and wondrously adorned the grand
Cathedral, now the glory, peerless pride,
The matchless structure of the modern world.

    Not Dian's twice-built dome at Ephesus,
Whose very site Time's blinding dust hath hid;
Not Rome's cathedral, heavenward pillared high,
Like arch of glory raised above the tomb

Of saint low slumbering in the earth beneath;
Not these combined with all the trophies won
By earthly art could with Truth's Temple vie.
In length or breadth, in loftiness or depth,
In beauty, grandeur or sublimity.
Twelve lofty towers 'bove reach of mortal skill
Gleamed in th' eternal beams white as the snow ;
Seven fronts wide as a mountain ranged,
Whose pointed gables tapered 'mid the stars,
In arabesque wrought by immortal touch ;
Rich pillared balconies of purest gold
Environed all the Temple's vast extent.
The holy Temple bore upon each front
In blood-red letters the divine command,
By John the Baptist preached, saying " Repent
Ye for Heaven's kingdom is at hand."
Sev'n avenues into the Temple led
Symbolic of sev'n ages of mankind ;
And branching from these avenues, like roots
Of giant trees, were many thoroughfares,
By countless bands of advent pilgrims thronged,
From many sep'rate kingdoms of the earth.
   The Arch of Triumph crowned my entrance-way ;
And there an angel stood with holy book,
In which each advent must record his name,
From whence he came, and whither bound, belief,
And what he seeks to do and what to know.
Therein my name, "Phantasmagoria,"
I wrote ; and whence I came, the "Mortal World,"
And whither bound—the Great White Throne of God ;
My creed, that "God the Father made the world,
And me, that God the Son did me redeem
And all mankind, that God, the Holy Ghost,
Me sanctified and all the people of God ; "
"ARISE AND CONQUER," what I sought to do,
And what I sought to know, " should I, by Grace
Divine, inherit life eternal ? "
                              Then
The angel pointing toward the Temple, said
            " Go ask and unto thee it shall be giv'n,
               Go seek and thou shalt find, knock, and it shall
               Be opened unto thee. The Temple now
               Approach with trust in God and faith supreme."

   Within the Temple's courts were crystal streams
That wound meandering over silv'ry beds ;

And sparkling fountains cast their spray aloft,
To float in air like beauteous showers of pearl.
Seven angels at seven golden gateways sat,
Each on a massive throne, from blood-stone carved,
To warn the people of seven "mortal sins,"
And terrors of the Hall of Eblis, in
Whose dark saloons and gloomy corridors,
Forever wander with their hearts of fire
Sin's shallow devotees.
     The archway o'er
The entrance to the inner courts was called
The "ARCH OF ECCE HOMO," from the dark,
Grim masonry at Pontius Pilate's gates,
'Neath which our Saviour, crowned with thorns, and clad
In purple mockery of royal garb,
Was led by Pilate to the raging crowd,
To whom he "Ecce homo" cried, "Behold
The man," and thus to death delivered him.
Engraved upon the curving arch appeared
The new commandments, by our Saviour given
Unto the lawyer of the Pharisees,
Who, seeking to entrap or tempt Him, asked,
"Which is the great commandment in the law?"
And Jesus answ'ring said unto him, "Thou
Shalt love the Lord thy God with all thy heart
And all thy mind, and all thy soul: this is
The first and great commandment in the law:
The next is like unto it; thou shalt love
Thy neighbor as thyself. Upon these two
Commandments all the law and prophets hang."
 Uprising in the temple's very walls
This arch stood forth as a remembrancer,
That they must pass beneath the yoke of scorn,
And tread the vale of deep humility,
And bear the cross, who would at length, like Christ,
ARISE AND CONQUER with the sword of Truth.

 Within that temple, Lo! I saw reared up,
In color like to sun-illumined gold,
A ladder stretching to high Heaven from earth,
With countless rounds that flashed like bars of gold.
It from the Rock of Ages glittering sprang;
And nearest Heaven the ten golden rounds
Did symbolize the Ten Commandments given
By God, to man, from Sinai's sacred top.
Above each round the cross of Calvary shone,

On which, in figure fadeless and revered,
The blood-traced letters I H S appeared.
From the first round a voice spake forth these words :
"I am the Lord thy God, and thou shalt have
No other Gods but me." Each one of those
Ten rounds spake forth accordant with its rôle.
Above the fifth, commanding every man
"Honor thy father and thy mother, that
Thy days may be long in the land," stood, with
A flaming two-edged sword, the angel Death.

I saw the ladder flooded with a light
Ineffable, and countless seraphim,
In radiant armor and apparel clad,
Ascend and descend on the shining rounds,
And bid the poor in spirit and the pure
In heart, the meek, the lowly and reviled,
ARISE AND CONQUER in the Saviour's name.
For has he not to all his people said,
"Lo! unto him that *overcometh* will
I give to eat the Tree of Life, which is
The middest of the Paradise of God."

Above the topmost round Sandalphon stood—
Angel of prayer—petitions to receive
From contrite hearts, and bear them up unto
The Great White Throne and Him that sat on it.
I heard the dying with a loud voice cry,
As through the dark and shadowy vale of death
They passed, " O Lord, have mercy upon us."
These dying prayers I saw Sandalphon catch.
His hands transformed them to immortal bloom,
And bore their fragrance of devotion up
In viewless volumes to the Throne of God,
At whose decree the meek petitioners
Were set as stars within His firmament.

They who approach Truth's Temple doors, and would
The shining stairway climb within, must cull
Some typic armor out and put it on ;
For otherwise they might not dare attempt
To tread the upward-leading golden steps.
The armors in that temple's vestibules,
With quaint designs, rare workmanship ornate,
Bore each its own exponent and intent,
And chief among them hung the BLOOD-RED CROSS.
There was the armor which Bohemian Huss

4 DO

Wore, when around him rolled the fires of Hell ;
He who, while dying at the stake, exclaimed.
" The fire which you are kindling up this day
Will light all Europe!" God! whose smile divine
All Paradise with glory floods, whose frown
Like a thick pall of darkness lowers above
The overarching canopy of Hell,
Thy spirit did sink deep down in his heart,
Kindling a quenchless fire, which yet shall burn
Throughout the generations yet to come.

There too the blood-stained armor hung which proved
A shield and buckler to the mighty heart
Of Christian striving with Apollyon,
Like unto Christian's but with clearer light,
Shone forth the robe of deep humility,
Which wrapped the thief upon the cross, and bore
Him, that day, into Paradise with Christ.

God grant that, when the Judgment day shall come,
I may in armor of humility,
Like Christian, or the dying thief, upon
The golden stairs, Arise and Conquer, too.

The sons of earth thronged in vast multitudes
Around the Rock of Ages, pressing on
To gain admittance through the vestibules,
And climb the shining ladder to the skies,
Many bowed down in supplicating prayer
Invoked the blood of Christ, the Son of God ;
And thousands marching onward, glorified
Jesus in that impassioned hymn of faith
Whose harmony celestial ever rolls.

Rock of Ages, cleft for me,
Let me hide myself in Thee;
Let the water and the blood,
From Thy side, a healing flood,
Be of sin the double cure,
Save from wrath and make me pure.

Should my tears forever flow
Should my zeal no languor know.
This for sin could not atone;
Thou must save, and Thou alone;
In my hand no price I bring,
Simply to Thy cross I cling.

While I draw this fleeting breath,
When mine eyelids close in death,
When I rise to worlds unknown

And behold Thee on Thy throne,
Rock of Ages oleft for me,
Let me hide myself in Thee.

    *   *   *   *   *

Within the temple many courts appeared
With ornature of every land, but each
Transparent as fine glass, and each did lead
Unto the sacred way, bathed with the light
Of Paradise. Within each court I saw
The armor of the Blood-Red Cross, wherein
The sons and daughters of the earth might RISE
AND CONQUER at the judgment-day.
                          Upon
The margin of each court, a liquid wall,
As 'twere a polished mirror rose, whose depths
Were set with scenes imperishably wrought
From marble or from ivory, by some
Immortal sculptor in his studio
Celestial, by whose art omnipotent
The flame of life flashed from the eyes, blushed on
The cheeks, and quivered in the lips of stone.
The forms seemed sentient and the fields of green,
The golden streets, and gorgeous palaces,
With domes of silver, pinnacles of light,
Beneath a diamond-studded canopy,
All shimmering in light ineffable,
Mocked vivid nature by the semblance of
More vivid life in animated stone.
Yet in those mirrors by th' eternal fixed,
Eternal, changeless, ineffaceable,
These scenes reflected on the bordered courts
Their own conceptions of eternal life,
The essence and the grounds of faith, the rites
To be performed to gain the central court
Whence springs the golden ladder to the skies.
  Here, bending from the sky Madonna reached
Her mediate hand to lead her orators;
While bands of virgin devotees, and priests
In gold and purple robes, perpetuate
Upon their sacred altars taper lights
First by the ancient fathers kindled on
Their altars in the Roman Catacombs;
There, flowed a type of Jordan on whose banks
A multitude of worshipers attend,
While in the current stands a penitent
Led by the priest to wash his guilt away;

Here, in a forest, 'neath the canvas spread,
By glimmering torch-light, thousands worshiping,
While from the mirror's tell-tale depths is heard
An echo of resounding jubilee ;
There, staid and void of ceremony, stand
Unkneeling, unimpulsive, worshipers
As if fulfilling their immutable,
Eternal destiny, eternal fixed ;
Here, saints bowed down before the Great White Throne,
In endless anthems chant Jehovah's praise ;
Here, mid celestial mansions seraphs walk
On golden pavements, shining in the light
And glory of the Son and Holy Ghost ;
There, sailing on their gorgeous wings, come bands
Of singing angels with their golden harps.
    Within an ancient court whose avenue
Led to the Temple of Jerusalem,
I saw a gleaming light whose radiant shafts
Rose luminous around the letter

On the Mosaic pavement of that court
Whoever walked, bore on his face the light
Of knowledge unrevealed save in what beams
Of light that mystic symbol is enshrined.
I turned from this mysterious court and gazed
Again upon the Ladder of Light which from
The Rock of Ages sprang, and lo! I saw
Three shining rounds 'bove all I saw before,
Rising in order, FAITH, HOPE, CHARITY.
    One court still higher in antiquity
Appeared.   Within its mirrored walls arose
The fragrant incense of burnt offerings,
The flaming bush, and Siuai's thunderings.
But they who walked the pavements of this court
Had shut the entrance to the Central Court
And barred it with the cross.   Irresolute
Their hosts were strewn 'mid all the avenues—
A nation without country, scattered wide—
A principality without a prince.

A mirrored wall, its own distinctive scenes
Reflects upon the multitudes that throng
Each court, all trending toward the central court.
  Amid th' approaches leading up to these
Now gazing, I beheld thronged avenues
Extending far in tortuous windings, sprung
From chaos and in chaos vanishing,
Approaching near, but entering never in
The central court whence rose the golden steps.
Where'er they crossed the pathway to the straight
And narrow courts, the pavement stones were marked
With crimson stains and blanching skeletons.
Upon the mirrored walls that rose along
These avenues, I saw distinctive scenes
Which marked the faith, the hopes and destinies
Of the innumerable hosts that to
And fro were marching on the broad highways.
Here, rolled the car of Juggernaut, and there,
Flamed up the Hindoo widow's funeral pyre;

  The mirrored walls about the central court
No gorgeous insignia bore: simply
A cross,—token of sorrow, sacrifice
And death, price of redeeming love: above
A manger shone the Star of Bethlehem,—
Heaven's signal heralding a Saviour's birth;
Jehovah out of chaos forming worlds,
And all illumined by the Holy Ghost:
Creative Majesty, Redeeming Love,
And Sanctifying Spirit, Trinal Beams
Merged in one God omnipotent.
                                Within,
The Holy of Holies, the common source
And end, the central court and throbbing heart
Whence life and action thrilled the branching courts,
Was circled by celestial seraphim.
"Faces had they of flame and wings of gold."
Lo! from the empyrean fell a shining cloud,
And hovered like a coronal above
The surging masses in the vales below,
As in the summer night, above the vale
Of Chamouni, a silver-fringed cloud
Oft hides the moon whose argent glory still
The fickle cloud reflects, then breaks, and 'twixt
The rifted edges shines the full, round moon
In mellow splendor on the beauteous vale;

So broke the shining coronal of cloud
Above the Rock of Ages hovering,
And through the rift a radiant angel's face
Shone on the thronging multitude beneath.
Whence came down-floating on the heav'n-born breeze
Seraphic symphonies, whose blending strains
Recalled lost Eden's primal melodies.
Each rapturously sweet refrain with prayers
And praises of th' assembled angels teemed.
Oh! with what soul-ingulfing ecstasy
Rolled forth the notes of that triumphal hymn—

O, realms of the faded
  Past, glimm'ring and shaded,
That roll in the mists of the vanishing eld;
  The temples ye cherished
  Are crumbled and perished
By Time's surging billows that over them swelled.

Before the dark river
  Submerges forever
The jewels and gems that embellished your youth,
  From out your deep azure
  Yield up ev'ry treasure
To glow in the sanctified Temple of Truth.

Here martyrdoms olden,
  That witnessed the golden
Faith binding the sacrificed saints to their pyres,
  Shall glitter hereafter
  In every bright rafter,
And ring in the anthems of seraphic choirs.

Here corridors ample,
  Where myriads trample
On pavements of crystal, of jasper, and gold,
  Are bright with the garlands
  And trophies from far lands,
Which tell of the heroes and conquests of old.

Here idols and sages
  From realms of all ages
Pass under the test of Truth's wonderful rays,
  Like glittering treasure
  Disclosing its measure
Of gold and of dross in the furnace's blaze.

The splendors adorning
The first rosy morning,
When infant worlds sprang out of chaos and night,
  Here blend with the shining
  Of time's last declining,
In many-hued glittering haloes of light.

  Lo! here is the portal
  Which leads to immortal
Bliss, after life's seeming cold shadows of love;
  The TRUTH is the burden
  And price of the guerdon
Of entrance and flight to the regions above.

  Let all the high arches
  Resound to the marches
Of ages and spheres that are rolling along;
  Ring out, ye loud pæans,
  From æone to æone
Till shakes the high dome with the thunder of song.

Through the bright drapery environing
The crystal gates of Heaven flashed the New
Jerusalem, by angels circled round,
Bathed in supremest fulgency, the sole,
First, last, and utmost fount of radiance,
Whence all the gleaming glories hitherward
Passed through, were only borrowed glimmerings—
The source and end of all eternity.
  The city of the New Jerusalem
Of equal length and breadth and height, prepared
By God for his redeemed of every age,
Adorned, as for her husband, a young bride,
Was like fine gold, transparent as pure glass.
The walls of jasper clear as crystal shone.
In each of the four walls three sev'ral gates,
Each gate one pearl, white gleaming as the snow.
An angel stood at each of the twelve gates,
On each of which appeared inscribed the name
Of each of the twelve tribes of Israel.
The walls had twelve foundations, and in them
The names of twelve Apostles of the Lamb;
And the foundation stones were garnished o'er
With sparkling gems, and every precious stone;
The first foundation was a jasper stone;
The second sapphire; chalcedony, third;
The fourth a single pale-green emerald;

The fifth, sardonyx; sardius, the sixth;
The seventh, chrysolite; beryl, the eighth;
A topaz, ninth; and chrysoprasus tenth;
Th' eleventh was a jacinth, and the twelfth,
An amethyst, red as the sparkling wine.

I saw no builded temple there reared up,
For the Lord God Almighty and the Lamb
Were there the temple. And the city had
No need of sun or moon to shine in it;
God's glory and the Lamb were light thereof.
The gates of it shall not be shut at all
By day: and there shall be no night therein.
Proceeding from the throne of God and of
The Lamb, a river of pure water flowed,
Life-giving, crystal clear; and in the midst,
And upon either side, the tree of life,
Which bare twelve fruits, and yielded every month:
For healing of the nations were the leaves.
There no more curse shall be; but throne of God
And of the Lamb, whose servants shall serve Him;
And they shall see His face and bear His name.

A massive, snow-white cloud, in volume rolled,
Transfused with unimaginable light,
To adamantine hardness crystallized,
Rose midway in the golden avenue:
The radiate scintillations, flashing back
From floods of light upon the crystal pile,
In intertwining and unnumbered threads,
Seemed, as it were, a woven drapery,
That like a shining mist eternal hung
In shimmering folds about the gleaming mound.
The everlasting throne its summit crowned,
Whence waves the scepter of the universe.
The throne gleamed whiter, brighter, tenfold than
Its base of crystal cloud; and He that sat
On it was clothed with MAJESTY and LIGHT:
Monarch supreme on His eternal throne!

With Him incorp'rate and inseparate
His garments, Light and Majesty appeared.
His ROBE of LIGHT, surpassingly intense,
Pervading, flooding boundless space, around,
Beneath, with beams of glory matchless and
Ineffable, whereof th' immortal souls

Of men are but as sparks ephemeral,—
The source eternal of eternal light,—
With shining undulations, first illumed
The Great White Throne upon the crystal cloud,—
Thence shone throughout the New Jerusalem,—
Whence radiant, all the universe reflects
The fineless, matchless, and perpetual glow.

The HOLY GHOST wrapp'd great Jehovah on
His throne, for He had put HIS SPIRIT as
A garment on.
                    His ROBE of MAJESTY
Was power creative, through whose exercise
Jehovah is, and all created things;—
FATHER almighty, and supreme, whose breath
Is tempest, whirlwind, motion, life, and death:
Creator, mover and preserver of
The countless orbs that roll in boundless space,
Christ said, when on earth, "I have not yet
Put on my Father," prophesying that
Returned unto the throne imperial
Within the New Jerusalem, He would
Resume the ROBE OF MAJESTY supreme.
    Now on the central Great White Throne high raised,
Clothed with supernal light,—the Holy Ghost,—
Invested with primeval Majesty,—
Oh! holy, blessed, glorious Trinity,
Three Persons and one God! to whom, in mute,
Involuntary adoration bow
All things create, in Heaven and on earth.

    The colors of the rainbow, blending, played
In ever-changing pictures through the air;
Elysian fields the far horizon swept
'Twixt summits mingling with the ether dim;
The lofty domes and towers on either hand,
High as the mountain pinnacles of earth,
Seemed piled in grandeur by the Hand, that in
Their orbits rolls the everlasting spheres.
Through crystal windows I beheld bright eyes
Of angels winged and draperied for flight;
Then through the open casements saw them flit,
Light as the thistle-down on Summer's breeze;
Sweet odors from celestial gardens breathed,
And strains seraphic filled the mellow air.

Behold upon the golden avenue,
Two cherubim came leading like a child
A fallen chieftain tow'rd the Great White Throne.

'Pure was thy life; its bloody close
  Hath placed thee with the sons of light,
Among the noble host of those
  Who perished in the cause of right.'

Emerging from the struggling multitude
Around the Rock of Ages pressing on
To gain admittance through the vestibules.
Lo! one of mien extraordinary came,
His eye and brow the counterpart of Jove.
He moved through waves of sempiternal light
Which from the Rock of Ages rolled in floods
A prince of men!   His every action seemed
To lift him up, as if above the clouds
His normal and congenial theater lay.
I saw him enter at the vestibule,
And upward mount·in blazing armor cased.
Upon the ample folds that wrapp'd him round
Was many a gorgeous device enwrought
From music, painting, sculpture, poesy ;
But chiefly from dramatic eloquence.
The colors blending gave a beauty, strength,
And almost a divinity, as if
From personating kings on earth below.
Triumphant now he would ascend on high
To bear Jehovah's semblance in the sky.
  His gleaming armor seemed invulnerate ;
But nowhere could I see the Blood Red Cross.
In place of it I saw a human heart
On which the startling emblem, " TEKEL," glared.
He grasps the Heaven-reaching ladder now,
Imparadised with angels' breath, and mounts
The golden rounds that lift him toward the skies.
Far upward now, where all discordant sounds
Of earth are lost or blent in harmony.
Celestial music bursts upon his ear
From hosts seraphic, round the Great White Throne.
No barrier meets him as he soars aloft
Until he nears the round on which gleams out
That changeless mandate from th' eternal God—
" THOU SHALT NOT KILL!"

                     No hand that hath been stained

By brother's blood, may grasp that holy bar.
His palsied hand springs backward as he strives—
Pale horror on his Jove-like features spreads—
He turns in terror from his God's command ;
And, falling headlong from the dizzy height,
Like Phaëton, son of Phœbus, when struck off
The Sun god's golden chariot by the bolt
Shot from the hand of thunder-hurling Jove,
Is lost beneath the murky clouds below.

  * * * * *

Then through all Paradise resounding rose
Entrancing strains of melody ; first low,
Then higher, with increasing swell, until
From New Jerusalem, with mighty waves
Of music thrilled, a glorious volume rolled
To mingle with the music of the spheres.
Then following, as when a prelude ends,
Unto th' immortal harmony attuned,
A myriad angels and archangels raised
With cherubim and seraphim, in full
Accord, the Te Deum Laudamus.
"We praise thee, O God ; we acknowledge thee to be the Lord.
All the earth doth worship thee, the Father everlasting."
Oh ! grandest of all anthems ! passing sweet !
The very winds seemed thrilled and resonant
With air and words harmoniously blent ;
Now rising like the billowy ocean's swell,
And then receding like its ebbing tide ;
Expelling from the chambers of the soul
All lurking ghosts of Hell-begot desires ;
Subduing all the passions of the man ;
Rebuking the perturbed spirit with
Assuaging grace of præternatural peace,
The mind ennobling, making strong the heart,
Till each, who heard the soul-entrancing strains,
Resolved "I will ARISE AND CONQUER too."

  * * * * *

O'er all the scene a mighty curtain fell,
This curtain measureless, in breadth and height.
Trailing the shores of immortality,
Athwart the boundless universe of space
Depends betwixt eternity and time.
High-arched upon its shining field appeared
An azure dome, studded with stars, where shone
The glorious sun in golden splendor, and

In argent softness the reflecting moon.
The golden sun, the moon, and twinkling stars
Were only scintillations flashing from
The Great White Throne whereon Jehovah reigns.

VALEDICTORY.

Phantasmagoria, daughter of the West,
Thou virgin child of fair Columbia! lured
By holy passion for the Spirit of Good
That woo'd thee willing on the dusky plains,
Thou didst conceive, in spite of low'ring clouds,
The grand design of making straight the paths
Leading from darkness of Delusion's wiles
To the immortal light of Faith and Truth.
By Mercy guided towards thy destiny,
Thy feet have trod upon the shining way,
And with the princes and immortal gods
Of ancient ages thou hast walked beyond
The confines of mortality, amid
The streets and temples of eternity.
True to thy birthright, 'mid the dazzling gleam
Of more than royal splendor, thou hast ne'er
Forgot thy mission—to illume the paths
By which we may ARISE AND CONQUER.
The germinating rays of wondrous light
In which thy pilgrimage has been baptized
Have giv'n to thy divine conception birth.
The clouds lift from the Mount of Faith, and through
The rifted veil glimmers the light of Truth.
From high Olympus to the Golden Star
I followed thine ærial journeyings,
And from beyond the shining portals flashed
Some glimmerings of wisdom on my soul.
Upon the fields of duty where I march,
May some effulgent droppings ever fall,
Kindling a flame of that ethereal fire
Which burns in moral heroism and warms
The heart to charity and quenchless zeal
In all that elevates humanity.
Phantasmagoria, farewell : I leave
Thee now to nurse thy offspring in the beams
That never fade, and warmth that never chills.

AMEN.